GUIDE TO
NEW ZEALAND

NEW ZEALAND

IAN GRAHAM

Consultants: Lois Huston, Robin Houlker, and Alan Lay

Highlights for Children

CONTENTS

On the cover: Milford Sound, on the west coast of New Zealand's South Island, is part of a World Heritage site—a place of international importance because of its outstanding natural beauty.

The publisher is grateful for the guidance of Lois Huston, a member of the management committee of the Children's Literature Foundation of New Zealand and librarian at Liston College in Auckland, New Zealand; Robin Houlker, an educational consultant based in Auckland; and Alan Lay, who holds a master's degree in geography and is the former head of the Humanities Department at Liston College.

Published by Highlights for Children
© 2003 Highlights for Children, Inc.
P.O. Box 18201
Columbus, Ohio 43218-0201
For information on *Top Secret Adventures*, visit www.tsadventures.com or call 1-800-962-3661.

10 9 8 7 6 5 4 3 2
ISBN 0-87534-575-1

EUROPE

ASIA

AFRICA

AUSTRALIA

New Zealand

ANTARCTICA

△ **New Zealand flag**
The deep blue background symbolizes the blue sea and clear sky that surround New Zealand. The four stars represent the stars of the Southern Cross constellation as they can be seen in the night sky. The British flag, known as the Union Jack, in the top left corner, shows that New Zealand has strong historic links with Great Britain, because many British people settled in New Zealand after it became a British colony in 1840.

NEW ZEALAND AT A GLANCE

Area 103,730 square miles (268,680 square kilometers)

Population 4,009,000

Capital Wellington, population 339,747

Other big cities Auckland (1,074,510), Christchurch (334,107), Dunedin (107,088)

Highest mountain Mount Cook/Aoraki, 12,316 feet (3,754 meters)

Longest river Waikato, 264 miles (425 kilometers)

Largest glacier Tasman, 18 miles long (29 kilometers)

Largest lake Taupo, 234 square miles (606 square kilometers)

Official languages English, Maori

▽ **New Zealand stamps** The designs below show some of New Zealand's many special-issue stamps. One promotes health through cycling, a second commemorates New Zealand's involvement in the America's Cup yacht race in 2003, and others show designs by New Zealand children for the 2002 *New Zealand Post* Children's Book Awards.

◁ **New Zealand money** The main unit of currency is the New Zealand dollar. Different notes show different famous New Zealanders. The 10-dollar note shows Kate Sheppard, who helped to win voting rights for women in 1893.

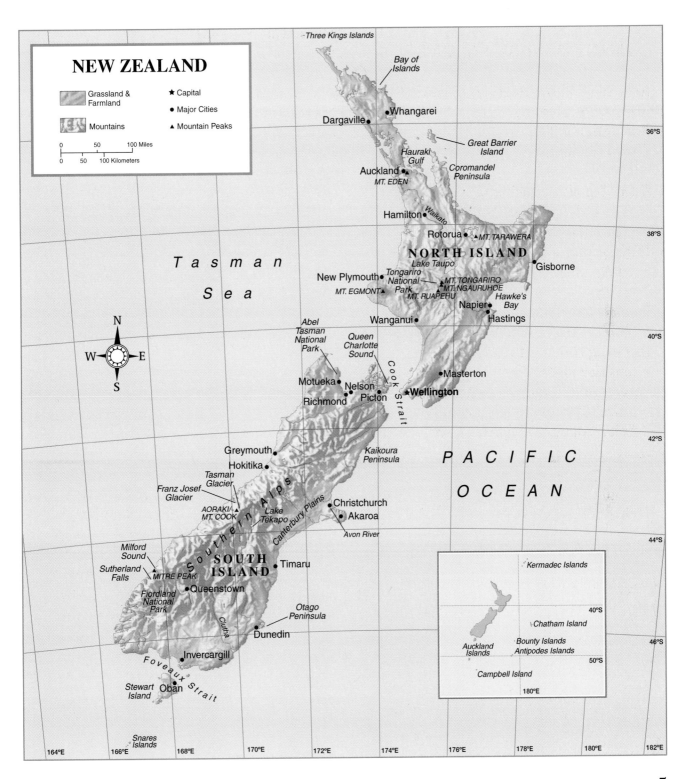

NEW ZEALAND

Grassland & Farmland

Mountains

★ Capital
● Major Cities
▲ Mountain Peaks

0   50   100 Miles
0   50   100 Kilometers

Three Kings Islands

Bay of Islands

● Whangarei

Dargaville ●

Great Barrier Island

Hauraki Gulf

Coromandel Peninsula

Auckland ●▲
MT. EDEN

36°S

Hamilton ●

Waikato

Rotorua ● ▲ MT. TARAWERA

38°S

NORTH ISLAND

Lake Taupo

● Gisborne

T a s m a n

S e a

New Plymouth ●
MT. EGMONT ▲

Tongariro National Park

▲ MT. TONGARIRO
▲ MT. NGAURUHOE
MT. RUAPEHU ▲

Napier ●

Hawke's Bay

● Hastings

Wanganui ●

40°S

N
W   E
S

Abel Tasman National Park

Queen Charlotte Sound

Cook Strait

● Masterton

★ Wellington

Motueka ●
Nelson ●
Richmond ●
Picton ●

42°S

Greymouth ●

Kaikoura Peninsula

P A C I F I C

Hokitika ●

Tasman Glacier

Franz Josef Glacier

Southern Alps

Lake Tekapo

Canterbury Plains

Christchurch ●
● Akaroa

O C E A N

AORAKI/ MT. COOK ▲

Avon River

44°S

Milford Sound

Sutherland Falls

▲ MITRE PEAK

SOUTH ISLAND

Timaru ●

● Queenstown

Fiordland National Park

Clutha

Otago Peninsula

Dunedin ●

Kermadec Islands

● Invercargill

Foveaux Strait

40°S

Stewart Island

Oban ●

Chatham Island

Auckland Islands

Bounty Islands
Antipodes Islands

46°S

50°S

Campbell Island

180°E

Snares Islands

164°E   166°E   168°E   170°E   172°E   174°E   176°E   178°E   180°E   182°E

5

LAND OF THE LONG WHITE CLOUD

New Zealand is one of the world's most isolated nations. It lies about 1,000 miles (1,600 kilometers) southeast of Australia, with the Tasman Sea to the west and the southern Pacific Ocean to the east. There are two large islands, the North Island and the South Island, and several smaller islands. The country's isolation has allowed a unique variety of plants and animals to develop there, including the national bird, the flightless kiwi. New Zealanders often call themselves by the nickname of Kiwis, after the distinctive little bird.

New Zealand was the last of the large land areas on earth to be inhabited by people. It was not discovered until about 1,200 years ago. Polynesian people were the first to arrive. Their descendants form the country's Maori population today. According to legend, the great Polynesian explorer Kupe named New Zealand *Aotearoa* (the Land of the Long White Cloud). Maori have their own distinctive culture and language, which they are keen to preserve. You can visit traditional Maori villages and see Maori songs and dances being performed.

European explorers first discovered New Zealand in 1642. In the late 1700s, European settlers arrived to hunt for whales and seals. Today, most of New Zealand's people are of European descent.

New Zealand is about the same size as the United Kingdom or the U.S. state of Colorado. There are many fewer people than in the United Kingdom, while the population is similar to that of Colorado. Nearly half of the more than 4 million New Zealanders live in only three cities: Auckland, Wellington, and Christchurch. Large parts of the country are uninhabited.

As you travel around New Zealand, you will see spectacular scenery. The landscape ranges from steaming volcanoes and glacier-topped mountains to lush rain forests, grassy plains, and golden beaches. The climate is warmer in the north and cooler in the south.

▷ **Maori culture** Traditional Maori customs, such as the greeting known as a *hongi,* as well as language, art, crafts, food, dance, and dress are preserved and encouraged today.

▷ **Passengers enjoy a thrilling jet-boat ride** New Zealand is world famous for its adventure sports and activities.

▽ **Sheep farming** There are about ten times as many sheep living in New Zealand as there are people. The sheep's meat and wool are valuable exports.

THE SEAT OF GOVERNMENT

The city of Wellington was named by Europeans, who settled there about 1840. Because of its central location, Wellington replaced Auckland as New Zealand's capital in 1865.

Downtown Wellington is smaller than many other capital cities because the steep hills around it stopped it from sprawling outward. You can explore it easily on foot. The buildings are a mixture of historic, twentieth century, and ultramodern.

As you walk around the city, look out for the distinctive Parliament building, the National Museum, the Botanic Gardens, the Karori Wildlife Sanctuary, and the birthplace of the famous New Zealand writer Katherine Mansfield.

The National Museum, *Te Papa* (which means "Our Place" in the Maori language), presents New Zealand's history, art, and culture in a mixture of traditional exhibits and interactive displays. The Parliament building is also known as the Beehive, because of its shape. The old government building opposite it looks as if it is built from stone, but it is actually one of the

△ **Wellington's cable car** The cable car has been carrying people between the city and the top of one of the hills that overlook it since 1902.

world's largest wooden buildings.

New public buildings, including the Beehive and *Te Papa,* are built on earthquake-resistant foundations. Wellington is built around a long, active fault line where two parts of the earth's crust meet and push against each other. This friction between two parts of the crust makes parts of New Zealand an active volcanic region. When the two masses of land move, they cause earthquakes. The ground under Wellington shakes as many as 15,000 times every year, but the vibration is

△ **Maori wood carving** Heads and spiral patterns are distinctive themes because they represent Maori legends and ancestry.

so small that it goes largely unnoticed.

Take a cable car ride up to the Botanic Gardens on top of one of Wellington's hills to see a spectacular view of the city and harbor. Or take a bus to the Karori Wildlife Sanctuary, a nature reserve on the edge of the city in which all the plants and animals come from New Zealand.

Somes Island, in Wellington Harbor, is another wildlife sanctuary. Its inhabitants include the tuatara, a lizard-like creature known as a "living fossil" dating back to the age of the dinosaurs.

◁ **Lambton Harbor** Wellington's buildings cluster around Lambton Harbor. Some of its old quayside warehouses have been converted into modern restaurants on the popular street known as Lambton Quay.

SUNNY HAWKE'S BAY

Traveling northeast from Wellington, you enter Hawke's Bay, an area that is well known for fruit growing and wine production because of its warm, dry summers and fertile soil. The region's main attraction is the city of Napier. Because the city was destroyed in 1931 by a terrible earthquake, it had to be rebuilt. Many of its buildings look similar, therefore, because they were all built immediately after 1931. Many are painted in soft colors and are in a style, called Art Deco, that was popular all over the world in the 1930s.

Take a trip south of Napier and visit the town of Hastings. It also was rebuilt after the 1931 earthquake in an Art Deco style, as well as a Spanish Mission style with plaster-covered walls and red roof tiles. If you go out to the coast at Cape Kidnappers, east of Hastings, you will find the world's biggest mainland colony of gannets. More than 10,000 of these large, magnificent seabirds nest on the rocky coast.

Head northwest to Taupo. As you travel, look out for the three volcanoes of the Tongariro National Park rising up on the horizon. Mount Ngauruhoe, Tongariro, and Ruapehu are still active. Steam and gas rise from their slopes and summits. Mount Ruapehu, the biggest of the three, erupts every few years. You can take a flight over the volcanoes and see amazing views of their craters.

◁ **The port of Napier** The attractive city of today grew out of the wreckage of one of the most powerful earthquakes to strike New Zealand.

△ **Tongariro National Park** New Zealand's first national park was donated to the nation in 1887 by the Maori, on condition that it would not be built upon or spoiled in any way.

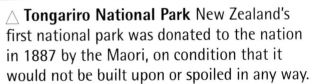

◁ **The Australasian gannet** These seabirds nest in huge colonies on the coast near Napier and Hastings.

THE THERMAL AREA

The city of Taupo sits at the northern end of Lake Taupo, New Zealand's largest lake. The lake was formed in the year A.D. 186 by one of the world's biggest volcanic eruptions. It spewed enough ash and dust to darken the sky. Today, the lake is popular with anglers, who fish there for trout.

New Zealand's longest river, the Waikato, flows out of Lake Taupo and then heads north. Hydroelectric power stations on the Waikato River can generate up to 25 percent of the nation's peak electricity demands.

Take the Thermal Explorer Highway to Rotorua. This part of the North Island is called the Thermal Area because there is so much volcanic activity. Geysers of boiling water spout high in the air, steam hisses from cracks in the earth, pools of hot mud bubble and boil. Few plants can survive in the harsh landscape, but brightly colored mineral deposits make up for the lack of flowers. Some of the lakes are brightly colored, too, because of minerals dissolved in the water.

Maori settlers used the hot springs for cooking and washing. Food can still be cooked in them today.

△ **Cultural traditions** A Maori male performs a *haka*, which was once a war challenge. The Maori take part in traditional dances, songs, and crafts, such as carving and weaving, at the Maori Arts and Crafts Institute in Rotorua.

Visit a Maori cultural performance at one of the area's traditional Maori villages. You can see Maori women dance using *poi*, small balls on cords that are swung around the body.

When Mount Tarawera erupted violently in 1886, three Maori villages built nearby were buried under the ash. One of them, Te Wairoa, has recently been dug out of the ash, and now you can visit it. Today, it is known simply as the Buried Village. It has excellent displays and relics that came from the area of the Mount Tarawera eruption. It is just like being in a Maori village in the 1800s.

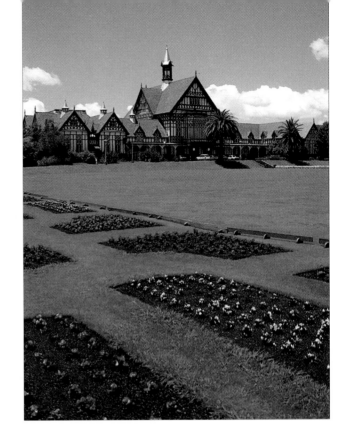

△ **Rotorua Museum of Art and History** In the museum you can find displays of carvings by the local Arawa Maori people, samples of traditional Maori tattooing, and information about the 1886 eruption of Mount Tarawera.

◁ **Whakarewarewa Thermal Reserve** The steaming, boiling mud pools of Whaka, as local people know it, are at the south end of Rotorua city.

13

HARBOR CITY

Head northwest to Auckland, New Zealand's biggest city. Auckland's Waitemata Harbor is a popular base for sailboats and motor boats and is packed with hundreds of yachts. The harbor looks out onto the Hauraki Gulf, where the America's Cup yacht races were held in 2000 and 2003.

The city's museums and landmarks include the 1,076-foot-high (328-meter) Sky Tower, the National Maritime Museum, the Auckland Museum, and the Museum of Transport, Technology, and Social History (MOTAT). The city also has a zoo, where you can see examples of Australasian wildlife as well as animals from other continents.

Auckland was the birthplace of Sir Edmund Hillary. With the Nepalese mountaineer Tenzing Norgay, Hillary was the first person to climb Mount Everest, the world's highest mountain, in 1953.

Auckland stands on a narrow neck of land, called the Tamaki Isthmus, between

△ **America's Cup success** New Zealand won the America's Cup, the world's most important yacht-racing trophy, for the first time in 1995. It won again in 2000, the first successful defense of the cup outside the United States in 150 years.

▷ **Hot Water Beach, Coromandel Peninsula** A favorite pastime is to dig a hole in the sand and lie in a natural bath as hot water bubbles up to the surface.

▽ **Auckland** New Zealand's largest city is the only one in the nation with a population greater than 1 million.

the Hauraki Gulf and the Tasman Sea. You can hike from one side of the isthmus to the other. If you follow the Coast-to-Coast Walkway and include a visit to the summit of Mount Eden, Auckland's highest volcano, the trip takes about four hours.

Across the Hauraki Gulf from Auckland, the Coromandel Peninsula is a popular North Island vacation spot. Gold was discovered here in the 1880s. At Hot Water Beach, south of Hahei, springs of hot water boil up through the sand.

The Bay of Islands, north of Auckland on the east coast, is a subtropical paradise of more than 100 islands. On the coast of the bay, you will find Waitangi, a famous name in New Zealand's history. This is the place where the Treaty of Waitangi, which founded modern New Zealand, was signed in 1840 by the United Kingdom and New Zealand's Maori tribes.

15

HEADING SOUTH

From Wellington, cross Cook Strait, the narrow stretch of water between the North and South Islands. The journey to Picton or Nelson at the top of the South Island takes between two and three hours by ferry or just 30 minutes by air. The strait is named after Captain James Cook, the English explorer who visited New Zealand and mapped its coast in 1769–1770.

During the ferry trip, look out for Arapawa Island. According to a Maori legend, this is the place where the Polynesian explorer Kupe caught an octopus he had chased across the Pacific Ocean and so discovered New Zealand.

The Cook Strait ferries reach land on South Island at the pretty town of Picton. This small waterfront town stands at the head of Queen Charlotte Sound, one of the Marlborough Sounds. *Sound* is the name given here to the flooded valleys that carve this coast into long channels, bays, and islands. The sheltered waters of the sounds are ideal for salmon and mussel farming and are also a great place to go sea kayaking.

Before heading south, take a trip westward along the coast through the towns of Nelson, Richmond, and Motueka, stopping off at some of the arts and crafts shops and art galleries on the way. The coast road from Richmond to Motueka passes Rabbit Island, a popular picnic spot with public barbecues and a sandy beach.

Further on beyond Motueka is the Abel Tasman National Park, situated on the coast between Tasman Bay and Golden Bay. The park was opened in 1942, exactly 300 years after the Dutch navigator Abel Tasman first sailed into the strait and sighted the land. Its varied scenery ranges from golden beaches to dense bush rising steeply up more than 3,280 feet (1,000 meters) above sea level. Walking trails crisscross the park.

▽ **Craft shops** Many painters, potters, wood-carvers, and sculptors are based in or near Nelson. Their work is displayed in the many galleries and craft shops in the area.

Sea kayaking The most adventurous of the sea kayakers in this area paddle out of the Marlborough Sounds and into the Tasman Sea itself.

▽ **Marlborough Sounds** Subtropical trees and shrubs cover the slopes of the flooded valleys that form the coastline of South Island at Cook Strait.

17

CITY OF GARDENS

On the way to Christchurch, take a break from the five-hour drive down State Highway 1 by stopping off at the Kaikoura Peninsula. The Kaikoura mountain ranges rise steeply from the coast. *Kaikoura* means "to eat crayfish" in the Maori language. Crayfish are still caught locally today.

The first Europeans to settle in this area of New Zealand were whalers, and whales can still be seen off the coast. Sperm whales pass by all year round, and humpback whales appear in June and July.

△ **An orca surfaces off the Kaikoura coast**
Orcas are attracted to the Kaikoura Peninsula because its seal colony, the largest on South Island, is a ready source of food.

Killer whales, or orcas, can be seen between December and February.

Christchurch is the biggest city on the South Island and the capital of the Canterbury region. It was formed as an Anglican (Church of England) community in 1850 by members of Christ Church College, Oxford, England. It still has the character of a traditional English city, with the tree-lined Avon River flowing through beautiful gardens.

The central area of Christchurch is compact and easily explored on foot or by bus or tram. You can also take a punt (a flat-bottomed boat) down the river to discover the city at a more leisurely pace. The center of the city is dominated by its stone Gothic cathedral in Cathedral Square. Many of the surrounding streets are named after English cities. Most of the streets are arranged in a grid pattern running north-south and east-west. The whole central area lies within four avenues that form a rectangle. Hagley Park and the Botanic Gardens cover most of the city's west side. Hagley Park is the biggest of the city's 750 parks.

Head out onto the Banks Peninsula. It was named after the English botanist Joseph Banks, who accompanied Captain Cook on his 1769 voyage. The small town of Akaroa was settled by the French in the early 1800s. Their influence can still be seen in some of the town's older buildings.

◁ **A tram follows its route along New Regent Street** One of the easiest ways to get around Christchurch is to hop on and off the city's trams.

▽ **Punting on the Avon River** As people lazily float past drooping willow branches against a background of gardens and traditional English buildings, they can see that Christchurch looks like part of old England.

THE CLOUD PIERCER

From Christchurch, continue southward across the vast Canterbury Plains, New Zealand's largest expanse of flat land. The plains formed when silt from the island's mountainous backbone, the Southern Alps, was washed down by rain. As you cross the plains, you will undoubtedly see some of the country's more than 40 million sheep grazing on the land. The fertile soil is also home to cereal and fodder crops.

Timaru, on the east coast, is about two hours' drive from Christchurch. It was built partly from blue volcanic stone after a fire destroyed many of the town's wooden buildings in 1868. From Timaru, turn inland and look out for Lakes Tekapo and Pukaki. These beautiful lakes are colored various shades of blue according to the type and amount of sediment within them.

Beyond the lakes, to the west, are the towering snow-capped peaks of the Southern Alps. One of them, Mount Cook, is the highest peak in New Zealand. Mount Cook is officially known as *Aoraki* (meaning "Cloud Piercer") to Maori because its summit is often veiled in clouds. Always impressive, Mount Cook looks even more majestic at sunset, when its snow-covered slopes change from white to pink in the fading light of the setting sun. According to

◁ **Landing on the Tasman Glacier** The Tasman Glacier is so big that aircraft can land there as if it were an airport runway.

▷ **The calm waters of Lake Tekapo** The turquoise lake is popular as a location for water sports and fishing and as a stopping-off point before heading into the mountains.

a Maori legend, Aoraki and the surrounding peaks were once sons of Rangi, the Sky Father, and were turned to stone when their canoe hit a reef.

Many of the mountain lakes are fed by meltwater from glaciers, which are giant rivers of ice that move slowly downhill. The Tasman Glacier on the eastern side of Mount Cook is by far the largest ice flow in the Southern Hemisphere outside Antarctica. You can reach the Tasman, Mueller, and Hooker Glaciers on foot from Mount Cook Village. Further west, the Fox and Franz Josef Glaciers sweep down the steep sides of the Southern Alps, almost as far as the sea.

△ **Aoraki/Mount Cook** New Zealand's highest mountain was 12,346 feet (3,764 meters) high until 1991, when a landslide reduced its height by 30 feet (10 meters).

THE PLACE OF GREENSTONE

Queenstown is a major tourist attraction standing on the shore of Lake Wakatipu, the third-biggest lake in New Zealand. Follow the S-shaped lake to Glenorchy at its northern end. From there, you can explore the wild lands of the west coast by one of the area's many hiking trails.

In the southwest corner of South Island are many flooded, glacier-carved valleys set between long fingers of land. They look like Scandinavian fiords, and so the area is called Fiordland. It is the least-explored part of New Zealand and the biggest of the country's 14 national parks. The rainfall here is much higher than on the east side of the mountains. Parts of Fiordland receive up to eight times as much rain as the Canterbury Plains. This huge amount of rainfall produces a lush rain forest that clings to the rocky coastline like a permanently wet, green cloak.

Milford Sound, the most northerly of the fiords, is dominated by a triangular mountain called Mitre Peak. It's named for its shape—like that of a bishop's hat, or mitre. If you follow the Milford Track at the head of the sound, you will see the dramatic Sutherland Falls, New Zealand's highest

▷ **Dolphins at play** Dolphins often swim alongside the boats that cruise Milford Sound. They race ahead of the ships' bow waves, leaping at the sea's surface.

△ **Spectacular scenery** Milford Sound, home to Mitre Peak, is one of the world's most impressive—and wettest—tourist spots. Up to 23 feet (7 meters) of rain falls every year.

waterfall. Visitors can cruise down Milford Sound and out into the Tasman Sea. The cruise boats usually pass the spectacular Stirling Falls, which drops 480 feet (146 meters) straight into the sea.

The Fiordland, Mount Cook, Westland, and Mount Aspiring National Parks form a massive World Heritage Area. This is a place of international importance because of its outstanding natural beauty.

The whole South Island is called *Te Wāhipounamu,* which means the "Place of Greenstone." Greenstone is a type of semi-precious stone that was collected by Maori from the swift-flowing rivers of the west coast. They carved it into tools, war clubs, and jewelry. Few Maori settled here. The steady rains and many insects in the region made it an uncomfortable place to live.

△ **Water and spray** The Sutherland Falls in Fiordland is the fourteenth-highest in the world. The water drops 1,904 feet (580 meters) and bursts into a cloud of spray as it hits the ground.

GOLD COUNTRY

A five-hour drive on South Island from Queenstown through the Central Otago region leads to Dunedin, the capital of Otago Province. It sits on the Otago Peninsula, extending from the east coast into the Pacific Ocean. Because the city was founded in 1848 by the Scottish Free Church, it has many Scottish connections. *Dunedin* is the old name for Scotland's capital city, Edinburgh. Dunedin is also known in New Zealand as the "Edinburgh of the South."

At the center of Dunedin, you will see

▽ **Main street in Arrowtown** In Gold Country, towns such as Arrowtown have preserved their historic buildings, which are a popular tourist attraction.

an eight-sided, tree-lined green called the Octagon. A statue of the famous Scottish poet Robert Burns stands in the middle surrounded by historic buildings. Among them are the imposing Municipal Chambers, Dunedin Public Art Gallery, and St. Paul's Cathedral.

A few blocks northeast of the Octagon, you will find the University of Otago, New Zealand's first university. It was founded in 1869 and opened in 1871. Today, its 13,000 students give Dunedin a lively feeling.

The Otago Peninsula is known for its variety of wildlife. Colonies of penguins, seals, and seabirds live around its coasts. You will discover most of them around Taiaroa Head, at the northern tip of the peninsula. There, you will see the world's only mainland colony of Royal Albatrosses. The Royal Albatross is one of the world's biggest seabirds, with a wingspan of up to 11½ feet (3.5 meters). Like all albatrosses, it rides the winds along the coast for hours on end.

Central Otago is Gold Country. Gold was discovered there in the 1860s. More than 20 historic gold-mining sites are linked together by the Otago Goldfields Heritage Trail. Towns along the trail take turns to hold events that celebrate the area's gold-mining history. You can visit restored mines and buildings and even try panning for gold yourself. Gold is still mined today in the red earth of the Central Otago hills.

▷ **Ancient rocks** Boulders and rocks along the coast of Otago are more than 200 million years old.

▽ **A bird's-eye view of Dunedin's Octagon** The Octagon green is a popular meeting place for residents and visitors alike.

LAND OF THE GLOWING SKIES

From Dunedin, the south coast is only three hours away by road. The road along the Catlins Coast gives the best scenery and views. It skirts the Catlins Forest Park and also passes the Cathedral Caves. These spectacular sea caves were carved out of the cliff by the sea's constant pounding.

At Invercargill, take the 20-minute flight over the Foveaux Strait to Stewart Island. Other travelers make the short journey from Invercargill to the fishing town of Bluff. There, they catch a ferry for the adventurous one-hour sea crossing to Stewart Island.

Stewart Island is the third-largest of New Zealand's islands, but it is tiny compared with North Island and South Island. It measures approximately 45 miles (72 kilometers) by 25 miles (40 kilometers). When Captain James Cook discovered it in 1770, he wrongly thought it was a peninsula connected to South Island.

Most of Stewart Island is uninhabited. Oban, at Halfmoon Bay on the northeast coast, is the only settlement. Boat trips leave from Oban's waterfront for the surrounding inlets and smaller islands.

Stewart Island is a bird watcher's paradise. It is home to the rare Stewart Island brown kiwi, a relative of the better-known kiwi found on the mainland. It is the only kiwi active in daylight. Within walking distance of Oban, penguins waddle between the sea and their nests in the brush. You

◁ **The tree-fringed coast of Paterson Inlet** Boats from South Island land at Oban, at the mouth of Paterson Inlet.

▷ **Boat sheds on the beach** Smaller boats on Stewart Island are launched down rails, which lead from sheds, onto the beach.

▷ **Sea traffic** Around Oban, fishing boats, water taxis, tour boats, and ferries make the waters busy at times.

might also see parakeets, the flightless weka, bellbirds, and the very rare kakapo parrot.

A stone building at Harrold Bay, within walking distance of Oban, dates from 1835, making it one of the oldest European buildings anywhere in New Zealand. Stewart Island's Maori name is *Rakiura*. It means "Land of the Glowing Skies" because of its colorful sunsets.

NEW ZEALAND FACTS AND FIGURES

People

People born in New Zealand make up most of the country's population. About 80 percent of New Zealanders are descended from Europeans. About 14 percent of the population are Maori. Asians, Pacific Islanders, Europeans, and other nationalities make up the rest of the population.

Trade and Industry

New Zealand depends heavily on trade with other countries. Most of its trade is with Australia, the United States, and Japan. New Zealand's exports include dairy products, meat, wood and wood products, seafood, and different types of machinery. Imports include vehicles, petroleum, electronic products, textiles, and plastics.

Forestry is becoming more important to New Zealand's economy. It supplies wood for manufacturing, construction, and timber exports. The timber industry mainly uses quick-growing pine trees from renewable forests, so that the country's remaining native forests

△ **The flightless kiwi, New Zealand's national bird** Before the arrival of people and their domestic animals to New Zealand, birds such as the kiwi had no predators. So they lost their ability to fly.

can be preserved.

The tourism industry is growing. More than 2 million tourists visit New Zealand every year.

The mining industry produces gold, silver, iron, coal, and materials such as limestone for the construction industry.

Farming

The success and wealth of modern New Zealand is based on the earning power of its farming industry. While manufacturing

and other industries have grown more in the past 20 years, farming is still New Zealand's most important industry. Dairy products are the country's biggest export. Dairy farming is the main activity for people who live in the rural areas of the country. More than 60 types of cheese are now produced in New Zealand.

In recent years, some traditional sheep and dairy farmland has been changed over to growing olives and grapes. In addition to traditional farm animals, such as sheep, cattle, and pigs, other animals, including deer and ostrich, are also farmed.

Fishing

New Zealand's fishing industry is also important to the country's economy. Seafood is another valuable export. About 600,000 tons (600,000 tonnes) of fish are caught each year. More than 1 million New Zealanders fish for fun and food every year.

Food

New Zealand food is a mixture of British, American, Mediterranean, Asian, and Polynesian influences.

Home-grown food is plentiful. Seafood is a specialty. *Toheroa* and *tuatua* (clams), green-lipped mussels, Bluff oysters, *paua* (abalone), snapper, eels, marlin, and salmon can all be found in the seas around New Zealand. Fruit and vegetables include the sweet, green-fleshed kiwifruit and the *kumara* (sweet potato).

Traditional Maori dishes are prepared at a *hangi,* when meat and vegetables are steamed for hours in earth ovens until deliciously tender.

Schools

Children start school at age five and normally remain in school until age seventeen. Higher education is encouraged at a variety of universities, polytechnic, and private training institutions. Language-based education is also encouraged. *Kōhanga Reo* centers provide Maori language for early childhood, *kura kaupapa* schools teach primary education in Maori, and there are *Wananga* institutions for higher education with a Maori focus.

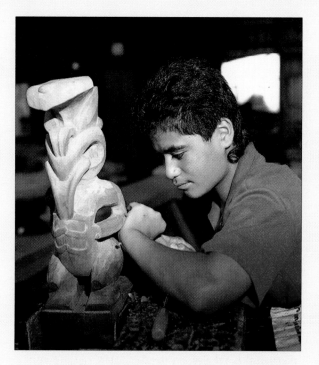

△ **A Maori wood-carver** Mythical creatures and human heads and figures are favorite subjects for traditional Maori carving.

The Media

There are 26 daily newspapers and about 700 magazines that are published in New Zealand on subjects ranging from sport and photography to home decoration and gardening. There are four national television channels plus pay-TV, cable, and satellite channels. More than 400 radio stations broadcast in New Zealand.

Music and Dance

The Maori people have a long tradition of music and dance. Unaccompanied Maori singing, called *ka mate,* often tells stories from Maori history. A famous Maori ritual is the *haka taparahi* war challenge. It is performed by the New Zealand All Blacks rugby team before international matches.

New Zealand has a national ballet company, the oldest professional dance company in Australasia; a national opera company; and a national symphony orchestra. Some of the cities have their own symphony orchestras.

Literature and Drama

About 5,000 books are published in New Zealand every year. Famous New Zealand authors include Katherine Mansfield, the short-story writer; Ngaio Marsh, author of the Inspector Alleyn detective stories; and Margaret Mahy and Joy Cowley, two well-known children's writers.

Seven professional theater companies and many amateur groups perform classical and modern plays. The largest is the Auckland Theater Company.

NEW ZEALAND FACTS AND FIGURES

Art and Architecture

New Zealand architecture is influenced by ancient Maori, Victorian-British, and modern international styles. The *whare runanga,* or Maori wooden meeting house, is found only in New Zealand. The first European architects in New Zealand designed buildings similar to the stone and brick buildings they had grown up with in Europe. Today, New Zealand architecture is as modern as anywhere in the world.

New Zealand has a lively visual art scene. Many art galleries can be found throughout the country.

Religion

About 60 percent of New Zealanders are Christian. Anglicans make up the largest group, about 15 percent. About 33 percent of the population do not belong to any religious faith.

Holidays and Festivals

There are national and regional holidays and festivals throughout the year. Local festivals are often held on different dates each year.

△ **Rugby match** Members of the All Blacks team wear black shirts, shorts, and socks with a white trim.

January **Wellington and Auckland Anniversary Day**

February **Nelson Anniversary Day**

February 6 **Waitangi Day**
National holiday commemorating the signing of the Treaty of Waitangi

March 23 **Otago and Southland Anniversary Day**

April 25 **ANZAC Day**
Commemorates the service of the Australian and New Zealand Army Corps in World War I

November **Hawke's Bay and Marlborough Anniversary Day**

Sports

Soccer (football), cricket, golf, and watersports are all popular, but the national game is rugby. The national team, the All Blacks, is one of the world's most successful rugby teams. Adventure sports and extreme sports, such as bungee jumping and white-water rafting, are popular with tourists.

Plants

Native plants range from kauri and kohekohe trees to ferns, sand-dune grasses, and the tiny alpine plants that carpet the mountain regions.

Animals

New Zealand's unique animals include the kakapo, the world's only ground-living parrot, and the flightless kiwi. Over time, many New Zealand birds lost their ability to fly because there were few, if any, predators to flee from. There are only two native mammals, both bats. Other mammals, including deer, possum, and rabbit, have been brought in from other places. On the shores are many birds and seals. Whales and dolphins are visible at sea.

HISTORY

The first people to discover New Zealand were Polynesians, who arrived in about A.D. 800–1000, and named it *Aotearoa*. The Dutch explorer Abel Tasman was the first European to discover the islands in 1642. It was the Dutch who named them *Nieuw Zeeland* or, in English, New Zealand.

The next European visitor was the British explorer Captain James Cook in 1769. He sailed around the islands and drew the first accurate maps of them. Cook and his crew marveled at the canoe-making and house-building skills of the Maori people. Whalers and seal hunters built small settlements around the coast from the 1790s onward. Christian missionaries began arriving in 1814.

In 1840, Great Britain and the Maori people signed the Treaty of Waitangi. This agreement founded modern New Zealand as a British-owned territory. The first constituted national government of New Zealand was established in 1852. Maori men were given the right to vote in 1867. In 1893, New Zealand became the first country in the world to grant women the right to vote. It was given more control of its own affairs when it became a British Dominion in 1907, but it still belonged to the British Empire.

New Zealand finally became fully independent in 1947. It also joined the Commonwealth, a group of countries that were British colonies but had become independent. In 1997, Jenny Shipley became the first woman to hold the position of prime minister.

LANGUAGE

The Maori language is the Polynesian language spoken in New Zealand and the Cook Islands. It is similar to Polynesian languages spoken in other parts of the South Pacific. There has been a written form of the Maori language only since 1815, when European Christian missionaries began writing it down. Maori use an alphabet of five vowels and only ten consonants—*h, k, m, n, ng, p, r, t, w,* and *wh*. Today, there are about 150,000 Maori speakers.

Useful words and phrases

English	Maori
zero	kore
one	tahi
two	rua
three	toru
four	wha
five	rima
six	ono
seven	whitu
eight	waru
nine	iwa
ten	tekau
Sunday	Rātapu
Monday	Mane

Useful words and phrases

English	Maori
Tuesday	Tūrei
Wednesday	Wenerei
Thursday	Tāite
Friday	Paraire
Saturday	Hātarei
dance	haka
food	kai
cave	tomo
stream	manga
mountain	maunga
Hello	Kia ora
New Zealand	Aotearoa
Welcome, enter	Haere mai

31

INDEX

Acknowledgments
Book created for Highlights for Children, Inc., by Bender Richardson White.
Editor: Lionel Bender
Designer: Richard Johnson
Art Editor: Ben White
Picture Researcher: Cathy Stastny
Production: Kim Richardson

Map and flag produced by Stefan Chabluk.
Banknotes from Thomas Cook Currency Services.
Stamps from Stanley Gibbons.

Editorial Consultant: Andrew Gutelle
New Zealand Consultants: Lois Huston, Robin Houlker, and Alan Lay
Editorial Coordinator, Highlights for Children: Joan Hyman

Picture credits
Corbis = Corbis Images, Inc.; EU = Eye Ubiquitous; JDTP = James Davis Travel Photography; RH = Robert Harding; t = top, b = bottom, l = left, r = right.
Cover: EU/P. Maurice. Pages 6: RH/Dominic Harcourt Webster. 7t: EU/Julia Mowbray. 7b: Corbis. 8l: JDTP. 8-9: Corbis. 9t: JDTP. 10: RH/Adrian Neville. 11t: EU/Terry Burton. 11b: Corbis/Kevin Shafer. 12l: JDTP. 12-13: EU/Paul Thompson. 13t: Corbis. 14l: Corbis/Onne Van Der Wal. 14-15: EU/Peter Kingsford. 15t: Corbis/Michael S. Yamasata. 16-17: Corbis/James L. Amos. 17t: Corbis/Robert Landau. 17b: Corbis/James L. Amos. 18: Corbis/Wolfgang Kaehler. 19t, 19b: EU/Paul Thompson. 20: Corbis/Paul A. Souders. 21t: RH/Storm Stanley. 21b: Corbis. 22: Corbis/Paul A. Souders. 23l: Corbis/Bob Krist. 23r: Corbis/Richard Hamilton Smith. 24: Corbis/Patrick Ward. 25t: Corbis/Anthony Cooper/Ecoscene. 25b: Corbis/Hans Georg Roth. 26: Corbis/Robert Holmes. 27t: Corbis/Kevin Fleming. 27b: Corbis/Robert Holmes. 28: RH/Maurice Joseph. 29: JDTP. 30: Corbis/Sean Aidan/EU. *Illustration on page 1 by* Tom Powers.